Little Red Riding Hood

Little Red Riding Hood is at home with her mum.
They're in the kitchen.
'Yum, Yum! What lovely bread!' says Little Red
Riding Hood. 'I want to take some bread to
Grandma!'

'Good idea! It **is** lovely bread!' says mum. 'Oh! And take some jam to Grandma, too!' says mum. 'It's in the cupboard.'

'Here's the basket for the bread and the jam!' says Little Red Riding Hood.

The sun is in the sky.

There are birds in the trees.

There are rabbits in the grass.

There are a lot of flowers.

Little Red Riding Hood stops.

She wants to look at the butterflies.

She wants to pick some flowers, too.

She wants to take some flowers to her Grandma!

'Oh! OH! A wolf! Behind the apple tree!' says Little Red Riding Hood. 'Help! HELP!'

'It's OK, little girl! It's OK!' says the wolf. 'I'm a good wolf. Who are you?'

'I'm Little Red Riding Hood' says Little Red Riding Hood. 'Who are you?'

'I'm … I'm Mr. Wolf!' says the wolf. 'What's in the basket?'

'Bread and jam. Bread and jam for my Grandma,' says Little Red Riding Hood.

'Where's your Grandma's house?' says the wolf.

'It's over there!' says Little Red Riding Hood.

The wolf runs to Grandma's house!

He knocks on the door of Grandma's house.

Grandma is in bed.

'Who is it?' says Grandma.

'It's me, Grandma! Little Red Riding Hood!' says the wolf. 'Please open the door!'

'Little Red Riding Hood?' says Grandma. 'No! It isn't you! It isn't Little Red Riding Hood!'

'Yes, Grandma, it is me! It's me, Little Red Riding Hood!' says the wolf. 'Please open the door!'

'Oh, no! No! It isn't Little Red Riding Hood!' says Grandma. 'It's the Big Bad Wolf!'

Grandma jumps out of bed!
She runs to the wardrobe!
She hides in the wardrobe.

The Wolf opens the door and goes into Grandma's house.

Grandma isn't in her bed.

Little Red Riding Hood knocks on the door of Grandma's house.

'Hello! Hello, Grandma! It's me, Little Red Riding Hood! Please open the door!' says Little Red Riding Hood. 'I've got some flowers for you. And I've got some bread and some jam in my basket for you. Please open the door!'

'Oh, Little Red Riding Hood! I'm in bed. Please open the door and come in,' says the wolf.

Little Red Riding Hood opens the door and goes into Grandma's house.

The wolf is in Grandma's bed.

'Hello, Grandma. Hello … Grandma, is it you? What big eyes you've got!' says Little Red Riding Hood.

'Yes, dear! All the better to SEE you with!' says the wolf.

'Grandma! What big ears you've got!!' says Little Red Riding Hood.

'Yes, dear! All the better to HEAR you with!!' says the wolf.

'Grandma! Grandma! What a big mouth you've got!!!' says Little Red Riding Hood.

'Yes, dear! All the better to EAT you with!!!' says the wolf.

'Help! Help! Where's my Grandma? Where's my Grandma? says Little Red Riding Hood. 'The big bad wolf is in my Grandma's bed. Help! HELP!'

Little Red Riding Hood runs to the door.
The wolf runs after Little Red Riding Hood!

Little Red Riding Hood runs into the garden.

She sees a woodcutter.

'Help! Help! Mr Woodcutter, please help me! Grandma isn't in the house! The big bad wolf is in Grandma's house!' says Little Red Riding Hood.

The woodcutter sees the wolf.

'Go away, you big bad wolf! Go away!' says the woodcutter.

'Thank you, Mr Woodcutter! But where's my Grandma?' says Little Red Riding Hood.

'Let's look in the house!' says the woodcutter.

Little Red Riding Hood and the woodcutter go into the house.

'I'm in the wardrobe! Open the door! Open the door!' says Grandma.

Little Red Riding Hood and the woodcutter open the wardrobe door.

Grandma comes out.

'Now let's have the bread and jam!' says Grandma.

Little Red Riding Hood, Grandma and the woodcutter all sit down.

'Mmm! I love bread and jam!' says Little Red Riding Hood.

1 Look and read. Put a tick (✓) or a cross (✗) in the box.

Example: This is a cupboard. ✓

This is a bed. ✗

1. This is a basket. ☑

2. This is jam. ☒

3. This is grass. ☑

4. This is a tree. ☑

5. This is a house. ☑

6. This is a bird. ☒

2 Read and colour.

Example: Colour Little Red Riding Hood's
top red.
1. Colour the basket yellow.
2. Colour the wolf brown.
3. Colour the bird in the tree blue.
4. Colour the flowers under the tree pink.
5. Colour the butterflies yellow and green.
6. Colour the tree green and brown.

Find the words

3 **There are five words in the circle. One is 'bread'. Can you find the other four?**

4 **Look at pages 4 and 5. Circle the correct answer.**

1. How many rabbits are there?

Three   Six   Eight

2. How many birds are there?

Five   Six   Seven

3. How many butterflies are there?

Eight   Ten   Twelve

4. How many flowers are there?

Eleven   Thirteen   Fifteen

5. How many trees are there?

Nine   Ten   Eleven

5 Make a paper bag wolf puppet. You need:

a paper bag

glue

scissors

crayons or pens

1. Follow the dotted lines. Fold and stick the edges of the bag.

This is the wolf's head.

2. Draw the wolf's eyes and nose.

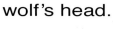

3. Cut out the ears.

Fold and stick them on the wolf's head.

6 Join the numbers from 1 to 20 and write the name of the animal.

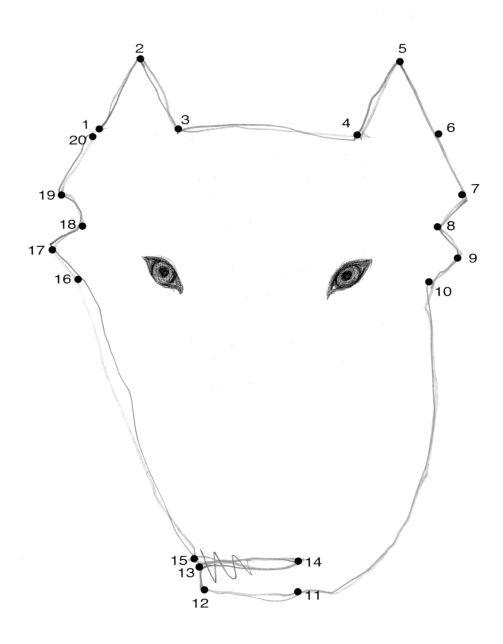

7 Find the hidden words.

rabbit   jam   red   basket   door
river   bird   bread   cupboard
butterfly   wolf   house   flower

```
r a b b i t e w c j x z
e w j a s b m o y a p q
d z m s y k a l b m s h
w r y k i p k f f s z c
b m q e e w t u o p l r
v f f t h g d o o r i i
f l o w e r b l g b e v
b r e a d d g t f i y e
v r f h k i d g g r x r
a q c u p b o a r d j b
q b u t t e r f l y c l
w c f k p l h o u s e a
```

8 Draw a line from the word to the object. Then write the word under the object.

river   flower   rabbit   butterfly

....

9 Join the jigsaw words.

4	do	ma
	ho	or
	b	robe
	ward	ed
	Grand	use

1 ....

2 ....   3 ....   4 _door_..........   5 ....

Picture dictionary

flower :

garden :

grass :

sky :

sun :

tree :

bird :

butterfly :

rabbit :

wolf:

girl :

mum :

Grandma :

woodcutter:

ears :

eyes :

mouth :

basket :

bed :

cupboard :

eat :

door :

hear :

house :

hide :

kitchen :

jump :

knock :

wardrobe :

open :

bread :

run :

jam :

see :

behind :

sit down :

Key

Activity 1: **1.** ✓; **2.** ✗; **3.** ✗; **4.** ✓; **5.** ✓; **6.** ✗.

Activity 3: jam   basket   rabbit   bird

Activity 4: **1.** three; **2.** five; **3.** ten; **4.** thirteen; **5.** eleven

Activity 7:

r	a	b	b	i	t	e	w	c	j	x	z
e	w	j	a	s	b	m	o	y	a	p	q
d	z	m	s	y	k	a	l	b	m	s	h
w	r	y	k	i	p	k	f	f	s	z	c
b	m	q	e	e	w	t	u	o	p	l	r
v	f	f	t	h	g	d	o	o	r	i	i
f	l	o	w	e	r	b	l	g	b	e	v
b	r	e	a	d	d	g	t	f	i	y	e
v	r	f	h	k	i	d	g	g	r	x	r
a	q	c	u	p	b	o	a	r	d	j	b
q	b	u	t	t	e	r	f	l	y	c	l
w	c	f	k	p	l	h	o	u	s	e	a

Activity 8:

rabbit   butterfly   river   flower

Activity 9: **1.** house; **2.** Grandma; **3.** wardrobe; **4.** door; **5.** bed

Editor: Robert Hill

Design and art direction: Nadia Maestri

Computer graphics: Simona Corniola

First edition : January 2006

We would be happy to receive your comments and suggestions, and give you any other information concerning our material.
editorial@blackcat-cideb.com
www.blackcat-cideb.com / www.cideb.it

CISQ CERT
TEXTBOOKS AND
TEACHING MATERIALS
The quality of the publisher's
design, production and sales processes has
been certified to the standard of
UNI EN ISO 9001

ISBN 88-530-0479-7   Book
ISBN 978-88-530-0479-6   Book

Printed in Italy by Litoprint, Genoa